AF603843

Claudia Chávez

LETRA

LOVE AND SUGAR FOR EVERY TEAR

Información del editor:

Editado por Letra
de Carlos Eduardo Caguana Sucre
Jr. Pedro Hearud 257, Barranco 15049 – Lima, Perú
Abril 2021
contacto@letragrupoeditorial.com
www.letragrupoeditorial.com

Diagramación: Andrea Vallejos

1era Edición, abril 2021

Edición digital – eBook

Publicado en Amazon.com

Hecho el Depósito Legal en la Biblioteca Nacional del Perú N° 2022-03666
ISBN: 978-612-5045-30-0

To María Sofía, my little flower and, my great joy, she teaches me every day how to become a better person.

And to Frank, the man who conquers my soul, I hope this love will last beyond death.

INDEX

Hot

Marriage is not a white dress

Love is not a thing of one day

I know you are not a saint

so, let's get undressed

and help me forget her

Now, your look is so sad

I need to understand

Why couldn't this be enough?

How do I know you like it?

shaking

how you appear in every shade

playing naked in my bed

but your acoustic isn't just for me

from this night, I'll let you be

You are my woman-guitar

I get excited with every string

play every silly thing

touching your curves

girl of my dreams.

Touching different parts of your body

everything is blurry

going down, underneath your clothes

asking me for more

breathing your breath

asking you: do you need me?

It was a Tuesday,

you were wearing your red skirt

and white shirt

red-haired and green eyes lady

everything happened very fast,

here are the facts

I am the teacher, you are my student

from reading a book to touching your knees,

kissing your lips,

fifteen years younger

after having you, I'm still hungry.

Good morning, babe

Yesterday was the first night

when I saw your stars

We made a full concert

play all your scales

up and down

Bet you are not human

Bet this is a nightdream

Just waiting a day to be the only one, dear.

I am a woman of the night

docile and, at the same time wild

you can buy my time, be yours tonight

give me caresses in forbidden places,

but falling in love can be a crime

be careful

having sex can be so lonely

but if you were what I need

you would have to share me, indeed.

Your black eyes

beautiful wise

on Tuesday, walking by the sea

on Monday, telling me you're leaving me

you will never know how much I cry, little liar

now you come with your curves and red mouth

dancing in my bed, making me the wildest sex

joining our eyes, feeling orgasms just like eating ice

that's the spell of your science.

Your breasts are sweet fruit for my mouth

I can't get enough of kissing your navel every night

and what is below that

although we belong to the same blood

dear cousin

feeling so weak

I don't want to stop

please, forgive me.

Your eyes and perfume

are like indelible ink

but you go away in a blink

should listen to my friends

don't give more than take

they said that woman is a nightmare

although, it feels so good in every taste.

Hope

There is life

after every misfortune

There is light

after every illness

and despite all your pain

love will always remain.

I feel defeated

every stone is a mistake

and there is no sun in the sky

then a voice whisper to me

take another path

built your own sunlight

over your crying nights.

yes, you can!

We don’t have control of many situations

life comes and goes

like the waves of the sea

it's best to let go, take a deep breath

the universe will do the rest.

Bad things really happen

we try to run away

but there isn't escape

So, think about today

you always have a new way.

Pain and hate are an avalanche

that cracks the soul stealthily.

They told us, you CAN'T!
But deep down inside
There was a defensive flare
antipode for the oppressor string.

We have the gift of raising a life

being judged by some

if we miss the train of age.

Listen again:

you can’t tell us what to do

you can't turn my life into blue

it is not up to you.

Please, don't leave me without your gaze

don’t leave in this losing game

I feel like a rag doll

so little that you can't listen to my call.

Woman,

fighter through life

always optimistic

Woman,

looking to the sky

unspoken elegance

Woman,

fire burns from your chest

poor disappointed man.

Be careful who you give your heart

don't forget scars will tell you who you are

Touched by this cold winter

walking with summer memories

trying to remember

how did it all begin?

It has been two months apart

Are we going to make it?

my heart beats too fast

seems I see your face in every morning sun

Holding on to your coat isn't enough

my lips miss you every Tuesday night

Frank, it could last forever

or it might be a short summer dream, however.

Self_esteem

I refuse to be an ordinary person

I want to be one in a million

be a pearl in a seashell,

and be a bird flying over Machu Picchu.

Stop listening to foolish opinions.

Little kid

listening to many "NO"

they don't know

you are afraid of those people

making you smaller.

Listen to your voice

you are the only owner of your fire

take one step at a time

there is only one life.

There is no purchase that cannot be negotiable

a nice house

rings and necklaces

but the train of life has no stops

thinking you were my savior

you were just a mirage

that send me a message

love cannot be bought.

Do what you love the most

Smile in every joy like the first time

and clean your tears with your hands whenever you need

Be grateful for every sun and moon

and calm your bad mood with a best sweet food.

Walking through the world

I found a rose

give her space

water with tears

love from my heart

becoming a nest was a start

One day I woke up

Discover the real rose

reflection of my mirror

living inside me.

It is easier to cure your wounds

but scars will continue

You can forgive

never forget

You brought me into the world

without love

I was a bird looking to fly away

I was a little girl begging for a caress

becoming a woman was a battle

now, far away

lucky me, love chases me

I raise my voice and face.

We can get ahead.

We can deal with these walking shades.

Woman, your story hasn't been
written yet,

you must paint with the watercolor of your lips,

build with clay
and outstrip

a new chapter worthy of your infinite eclipse.

My aching and heartbroken soul wanders

without your voice and way of smiling.

It's a fact that you are no longer here

and my mind dreams that you will return to me.

I won't let you fall apart

all I want to do is heal your broken heart

Why do you run away from the mirror every morning?

hey, this is a warning

nobody is going to love you as you do

nobody is going to feel pain for you

YOU, ONLY YOU, are all you need, dear youth.

Raise your voice

open your wins

you can do it, Louise

The past hurt you so much

but now the sea of tears

is healing with one touch.

Don't be afraid to look in the mirror

you are more than his lies

you are not an error, instead of a warrior

it is no more a dream

it is a prayer to be heard.

She let her flowers dry for you

shouldn't listen to people's murmur

Woman

why can't you realize how beautiful you are?

I want you to see what I see in your star

Taking your hand to save you,

you must try to find a way through

because this book belongs to you.

Infidelity

Your jealousy

isn't wrong

it reflects who you belong

at least four months ago.

Don't feel guilty

I just want the truth

who owns your nights

and who's the fool.

Don’t be an immature person

having so much love

but you have a vain feeling

look at the mirror

you are going to lose everything

just for a forbidden kiss

just for a fast souvenir.

Gabriel, how did you get into the score of my life?

You built my world based on melodies

and you sang a cappella the love you felt.

but it was a Friday without advice,

your chords were played by Ines

Out of time to escape

no compasses, no scales, and unfinished serenades.

After four winters

face to face again

no resentments, no illusions

all by myself and you with another girl.

The greatest man in the world

isn't a saint

isn’t a perfect match

although, transform my cloud into his breath

the greatest man in the world,

isn't affectionate

isn't a liar

but bless my day and dry my tears

even though our farewell was imminent

all the love you give me

is a treasure I will keep to survive,

although our worlds belong to different bodies

cause my greatest man pertains to other eyes.

You asked my permission to leave

Shame to know it was wrong, my dear Steve

Hungry and thirsty

for this repressed pleasure,

knowing it was all clandestine.

I only had brief memories behind

Well, every heart has another owner.

My dear, my all, and sweet James:

Your heart was broken so many times

reason for suppressing all your rhymes

Our personalities seem similar

you trust and let feelings burn again.

By the time you arrive home

I remember Tuesday in August

make you believe

I was with my best friend

Now in bed, we both breathe

guilty fragrance in the air.

I didn't mean to hurt you

it was more than joy

You were more than sex

but I'm just a bad girl.

You knew I would die for you

I was your wife

I was the only one according to you

Instead, you treated me like your walking puppet

Instead, you treated me like an old blanket

now, I can dry my tears

didn't know I was one of three.

Forgiveness

My aching and heartbroken soul wanders
without your voice and way of smiling.
It's a fact that you are no longer here
and my mind dreams that you will return to me.

I won't let you fall apart
all I want to do is heal your broken heart

I still know there is a light that is our eternal love

Could you come, my girl, and hug us?

To scale this cliff and together heal us.

Here I am at eleven-o-clock

on top floor

I swerved toward the edge of the precipice

waiting for a lifeline, still.

Oh, dear dad

I'm just only fifteen

I've never wanted to hurt you

I believed him and his errors

how to escape from this mess

but one thing I won't regret

it is the miracle of life

living inside myself.

Flattery

What a look

What a walk

my heart goes wild

when I look into your eyes

every time you pass by,

increase the heat

with your sexy smile

Every blink

I know you are watching me

and makes me think

can you give us a chance?

so, wait a little longer

you don't even know my name

well baby, welcome to this long love game.

I could become a dolphin for you

chasing my lost mermaid

my love will travel

deep oceans

lift every precious stone

and ask for a little reward

could be a kiss

could be a glance

all you can give me

Tonight, I will always be your soul

promise to be with you

I swear by the stars, moon, and your cold perfect nose.

September, the month you were born

the day I met you

walking through the rain

begging to the moon listen to my prayer.

Dreaming with your face so pale

how to tell those people, age isn't an obstacle

your heart and my soul just want to be a couple.

You are in every Chopin mazurka

and in every Becker´s poem

Drives me crazy at every movement

and every music you play

Let me be yours

Let me find you.

Hi,

let me introduce myself

it begins with an F of faith

and ends with an A of Amen

My name was born

the day I saw your thirsty lips

and whispered close to my ear.

I'm drawing your face with my favorite pen

memories of when we ever first met

I feel clumsy inside

just when you ask for my name

I feel clumsy outside

trying so hard not to fall in love like a flame.

I want to swim into your lips

breath your essence and eclipse

become one in an eternal kiss

I want to be more than just a date

I want to be more than just a friend

Dance with you

bring the moon to you

I hope God one day

listen to my prayer.

Even if I lost paradise

even if you stop loving me,

you are my madness and disease

I refuse to live without your lips.

Love could be my favorite recipe

it only requires a few ingredients

Starting with your black eyes

putting a kiss on each one.

Then, adding water

on your thirsty mouth,

cause *I can't live without you.*

Omit salt,

whenever you feel sad,

of your adorable tears

cause *I'll be there for you* through the years.

Set aside a few minutes

each time we are mad

to keep warm the flame

and whisper your ear

I adore you, my sweet dream.

Dissapoinment

A feeling I could fade away

every time you are playing games

you said I was the queen of your soul

when I was just one of your pawns

in your chessboard,

Now it is time

to let you go

baby, you know I gave it all.

On Tuesday, I sang
and undressed my scars
On table two in that little blue bar
If we had too many drinks
Let me tell you two things:

Do you still think of me?
Sorry, I forget that it would never be me, but
Would you give me a final kiss?

I was always there for you

until I forget about me

feeling so little

feeling small

like my old doll.

Being married

doesn't mean I have to love you

you are always in a hurry

and your eyes don't have the same shine.

Now I look at the sky

looking for love, one day we had

I can’t stop crying

we know no one was the bad guy.

In this fairy tale called youth
seventeen was the delighted number
fifty the number of our kisses
and three were the times I forgave your tricks

Enchanted by your lips
you were my guide and everything to me
the bloody fault we weren't free.

Now your sweet kiss has lost the magic
I opened my eyes
your charm has vanished.

You can handle the knights

as a morning craving.

You can wake up glances

full of wishes,

but what you will never be able to, beautiful lady

is to know true love

that strips the soul in a flight.

Sea of suspicion

divided by your simplicity and warmth

you could have run away

you could have told you goodbye anyway

instead,

you stay and listen

dry out my soul and tears

makes me paint pure and bright oceans

kissing my scars and healing my heart.

Death & Love

I just wanted a caress,

a gaze

a word.

Perhaps, a little more.

A slap,

a kick,

a torture,

all coming from you.

Tell me, mom, what did I do wrong?

Every day I left it all behind,

mom, can you change your mind?

painting your beautiful face

you turn me into the air.

Now, I am no longer here

There is no more pain or tears,

that's what the Lord said to me.

That day, the seconds seem like stilettos

and the hours without you, felt like a sadness *menuetto.*

God knows

I'd give my life for you

if only I'd go back to you

we knew

there was no guarantee

but your tired eyes calm

my tearful plea.

Amy, my beautiful young girl

love you inside and out forever

when I first met you

your lips drowned me with a big smile

and I realized you were hungry for life

Three years passed away so quickly

as quickly they sucked your passion and perfume

the pain was on the top

and agony blackout your soul

I truly believe death is not the end

I truly imagine your voice rumbles in the air.

Night sweats unveil my dream

I feel my cells dying, my body shutting down.

Lying on the bed, naked and bald, I try to escape, but it ties me up, punches my veins, my projects… my life.

I emerged and grasped the legs of the dungy crab and whispered: "Dear cancer, you won't beat me, you won't beat us"

Dear girls, you aren't alone

Many illusions in our childhood

Spaghettis and ceviche mixed with the sand on the beach

running with a friendly hand

taking soda not having that much

and the sun always follows our backs

Now every child has their family

begging not making the same mistakes

there were days eating only egg and rice

but through the window, you can reach the sunrise

Now I´m just an old lady

who yesterday buried her man

there were days with heavy rains

and others, sunny with his smile

Bet the death lady is near

bet I am going to see you again.

The air is touching my cheeks, it's you.

In your sleeping eyes, the hope that you will open them again.

In the silence, you look at me and I can listen to your words of inspiration with a gaze.

The pain ended with your exhale, you have gone to a better place.

The emptiness in my soul, I´ll fill up with your white eyebrows and mustache.

I want to go where you are grandpa, just to see you one more time.

See you soon, papito Julián y abu Carlos

Come on, my little boy

we met

the day the crab was under your sun

we built castles and forts

and for a year

the sky was really sunny and blue

Feeling guilty

couldn´t do more

Feeling angry

I couldn’t be there for you

Now, tell me how to feel when you are gone.

I don't know if any man could compare to you

but you were unique

kiss by kiss in my eyes

you wipe my tears

my hand in your hand guided my steps.

After twelve years

you are still the child of my dreams

little wizard,

we did not have enough money,

feelings abounded

After those ashes

only tears and resignation remain.

Days of nightmares

whenever I see you in pain

life doesn't prevent you from suffering

I close my eyes, I see you in the hospital room 205

getting away from this shadow.

Unpredictable situations in this travel machine

We can't explain them

only the fire of keeping us fighting

just you and I understand

the deepest of our ocean in each other eyes.

Misunderstood Love

I am tired to pretend

my name is Isabel

have a crush for Ines

today I am taking off this bizarre disguise

for many years trying to fit

who says this isn't love

if this feeling burns me.

I was a shy boy

who believes in good people and toys

nobody knows my secret

they say I go against the sacred

I remember when he took me by the hand

and said my name, it wasn't planned

mom, I just want to be loved,

regardless of sex, color, or race

mom, I am praying on my knees,

I just want to break free.

Do my woman wrinkles forbid us to love each other?

at my age, you could be my last lover,

fuck the judgmental faces

this might be one of many cases

but if you felt ashamed,

there is only one to blame.

Beautiful woman in her forties
sweet like an old wine
all the intelligence and wisdom behind
lazy man: stay away from her!
she is not just any girl
she is completely happy by herself.

Sweet fifteen

I will remember them forever

my first kiss

not everything is bliss

good and bad friends

don't think how much money spend

window to becoming a woman

being judged by other humans

remember your family isn't the bad guy

and it´s ok if nothing is alright

those tears don´t represent you

your heart will be the strength all the way through.

It was on November 18th

your sleepy eyes

bring me new life

you embroider every detail in the air

with every breath you exhale

you, the cause of my insomnia

you, little bird away from the nest

it is a white care

it is your black hair

it´s another kind of love

divine and odd.

Your black eyes

beautiful wise

on Tuesday walking by the sea

on Monday telling me you're leaving me

you will never know how much I cry

little liar

now you come with your curves and red mouth

that´s the spell around you.

While we were taking the exam

I was looking at your shiny brown skin

it was perfect as honey

perfect as the sun in the middle of the sky.

I was the nerdy girl

a faithful friend.

Today I thought after the break

reveal you this secret

but you and your friends suspected it

made fun of me

I thought it was the end,

but continue to be your help,

hopping someday, you will deliver me from hell.

Yesterday,

You convinced me with a rose

to be your muse

Every wedding

I dream of getting the bouquet

but after all, I was just a puppet

Today,

I choose not to choose you

Today,

cut the ropes that tie me to you

get my six senses back

and for you, leaving you my lovely revenge soundtrack.

So, I met you at the bus

after my first break-up

you told me you were a teacher

and how you play with children

you didn't know

about this empty cold heart

the truth is I used you to forget

only ashes you could get

I am really sorry, I swear

Today is our marriage´s burial

I hear the funeral march

instead, you listen to freedom bells

why the word love was so hard to spell.

Deep down you know that

isn't you who I love

when we walk together

in every kiss

I see ghosts

everything, even the air

reminds me of her.

Give you the little I have

with all my heart

Could be a commoner

Could be nobody

Why do people have to meddle

what they didn't know

we release our love

in a tear of satisfaction.

Friendzone Love

Becoming friends was the beginning
growing together giving us support
on the way, separation was inevitable
you only want to improve your score
and choose to become a sore.
Life gives us a new chance
destiny makes us meet again
however, chasing your ego at a glance
was your losing game.
Ten years passed in order to grow up
now I have a man who loves me back
but tell me, why I can't forget your sad black eyes.

Hey Mr. Tired Hands

I didn't have a crystal ball to prevent
you to invade my neighborhood, my steps
and soul, but it was my desire.

People really didn't understand
they only saw a man without money
where my eyes reflect a man whose hands
created his own world.

Your hands took me away from earth
you got the music and I had the lyrics
your hands molded a perfect shape in me
but you are still a friend to me.

Your eyes only have looked at me as a friend

the only way was to be a ghost between

your nights and days.

Yesterday, your lips spelled my name

Sara was all I ever wanted to hear

my red cheeks reveal how much I care

the longer you stay the more I am living with this pain.

I'm not sure if you are feeling the same way

it could be another kind of love

where I am the pawn and you, my king
but the game is going to end in checkmate.

Do you think that by marrying the other girl

are you punishing me?

You'll never forget those moments

when I gave you my soul

thinking it was a word called love.

I love you in silence

now I'm not going to hold back

I'll undress my feelings

and let my scars heal.

You only noticed me when

you thought you were about to lose me

guess what!

never had me

and will never have me.

Never talk to me

Never look at me

living in another galaxy for him.

Now he sees me

Now he talks to me

you are in my shoes but just keep trying.

Friends for more than ten years

many crushes between Joe and me

never told me a thing

but I knew he felt the same chills

I received a

message in the summer

Dressed in my little red skirt with

flowers

dancing

through my favorite dream

thinking on your blue eyes and

flying in the sky.

Looked out the window and waved at him

My heart stars on fire

my pulse was so high

there were two shades

you and the new girl, Mary Ann.

You knew I

gave you this power

to freeze my feelings

and cry you a river

now believe me, I am healed from

this fever.

January was the beginning of our relationship

just friends

so intimate

loving us was something innate.

I would not have asked you for that kiss

it was an instant of bliss

if I knew it was going to be the end

just friends we will remain.

Rony, today I climbed fifty steps

in the building where we work

just to get to your side,

my heart was on my lips

to declare how much I love…

you.

Saw you from afar with your shirt and tie,

taking another girl by the hand.

I returned to the first floor

where this wounded body belongs.

www.ingramcontent.com/pod-product-compliance
Lightning Source LLC
LaVergne TN
LVHW041043150826
845672LV00001B/442

9786125045300